HOTSHOT CREWS
ON THE SCENE

BY JODY JENSEN SHAFFER

Published by The Child's World®
1980 Lookout Drive • Mankato, MN 56003-1705
800-599-READ • www.childsworld.com

Photographs: AP Photo/Ringo Chiu, cover, 1; USDA Forest Service/Lance
Cheung, 5, 9; US National Park Service, 6, 14; USDA Forest Service/Kari
Greer, 10, 13, 16; USDA Forest Service/Cole Barash, 18; USDA Forest Service/
David Kosling, 20

ISBN 9781503855878 (Reinforced Library Binding)
ISBN 9781503856127 (Portable Document Format)
ISBN 9781503856363 (Online Multi-user eBook)
LCCN: 2021940169

Printed in the United States of America

TABLE OF

CONTENTS

FAST FACTS

What's the Job?

- A hotshot crew includes 20 specially trained wildland firefighters.
- These firefighters are called "hotshots" because they work on the hottest part of a fire.
- Hotshot crews fight fires with only the hand tools they can carry.
- Hotshot crew members must be physically and mentally tough.

The Dangers

- Hotshot crew members risk injury and death with every fire.
- Hotshot crews work in rugged, **remote**, and steep wildland areas.
- From 2007 to 2016, an average of 17 wildland firefighters died each year.

Important Stats

- During fire season, hotshot crews can work 24 hours a day.

- There are more than 100 hotshot crews in the United States. Most are in the West.

- A hotshot crew member earns an average salary of $40,000 during a six-month season.

Chapter 1

BECOMING A HOTSHOT

A firefighter in Prescott, Arizona, loved his job. He worked on an engine crew. He put on his gear and jumped into the truck when the alarm bell rang. He saved buildings and people. He was good at his job. Other firefighters looked up to him. But after doing his job for three years, he was ready for something different. He wanted to be part of a hotshot crew.

Hotshot crews are specially trained firefighters. They fight fires in forests. They fight the most difficult wildland fires. Most hotshot crews have 20 members. These crews travel from state to state. They fight fires in remote areas. The **terrain** may be steep. They may have to walk miles to get to the fire. Hotshot crews fight fires with only the tools they can carry on their backs.

◀ **Hotshot crew members have to carry all the tools and equipment they need for a job. They must be in excellent shape and work well in a team.**

The Arizona firefighter knew he could do it. But he would have to get in even better shape. He would have to pass a physical fitness test. It is called the Work Capacity Test (WCT). He would need to carry a 45-pound (20-kilogram) pack on a 3-mile (5-kilometer) hike. He would have to run a mile and a half (2.4 km). He would have 11 minutes to do it. He would have to do 40 sit-ups and 25 push-ups in less than a minute. He would do chin-ups.

The determined firefighter would also need to study and take classes. He would learn about fighting fires in a forest. He would learn about the tools hotshots use. He would have to pass written tests. Then he could finally apply for the job. It would be hard, but he was up for the challenge. He was ready to be a hotshot.

Hotshots create a fire line by clearing away ▶ brush and dead and fallen trees. Crews often work in very hot and dry conditions.

Chapter 2

A RIDGE ON FIRE

It was 2015. A Wyoming forest was burning. The fire was on a mountain ridge above town. Below the ridge, people, buildings, and animals were in danger. The town needed help. They needed to stop the fire. But the terrain was rough and steep. Firetrucks could not reach the ridge. What could the town do?

Chris Boyer hadn't really wanted to be a hotshot firefighter. It was the end of summer. He was in college. He ran into a friend who worked as a hotshot. The friend was muscular and in great shape. He looked healthy. Chris thought hotshotting sounded like a great summer job. He tried out and was accepted. He joined the Silver States Hotshots in Nevada. That was years ago. Now his crew was learning about a ridge fire in Wyoming. The town needed their help. The hotshots didn't hesitate. They got in their vehicles and drove to Wyoming.

◀ **A wildfire burns in the mountains of the western United States. Wildland firefighters work hard to prevent fires from reaching homes and buildings.**

The fire was hot. And it was moving. The hotshots had to get close to it. They needed to do a burnout. A burnout means setting a small fire around the main fire. This stops the main fire because there is nothing left to burn. It is hard, dangerous work. The Silver States Hotshots needed a plan.

There were lots of things to think about. They had to do the burnout when the wind wasn't too strong. They had to do it when the weather wasn't too hot. They were the only hotshot crew there. People were counting on them. They loaded their gear. They hiked toward the fire. They started their **drip torches** and began burning the forest floor.

Two days later, the fire was out. Chris Boyer and the Silver States Hotshots were heroes. The town thanked the hotshots, and the crew drove home.

A hotshot uses a drip torch to burn away ▶ dry grass and bushes. Removing some of a fire's fuel with small, controlled fires can help stop the spread of a wildfire.

Chapter 3

FIRE IN THE FOREST

It was 6 a.m. The hotshot crew had slept at fire camp. Fire camp was like a small city in the forest. It had showers and food. It even had toilets. But now the crew had gathered for the morning briefing, or meeting. There was a report of a fire in the forest. They needed to get to the fire fast. The hotshots got their instructions. They got safety information. They were told what ground and air radio channels to use. And they were told where camp medical services would be. This information could all be found in a report called an Incident Action Plan.

They grabbed their heavy packs and tools. The hotshots hiked into the forest. Their first job was to attack the fire by cutting a fire line. A fire line, or firebreak, is a strip of open land. The crew cleared the land so the fire didn't have anything to burn. They had to do it quickly. They grabbed their chingaderas. A chingadera is a hand tool that is shaped like a hoe and can be used to dig, scoop, and move debris.

◀ **Wildland firefighters meet regularly to plan how to put out a fire. They discuss the tools and crews they might need to help them.**

▲ A hotshot cuts through a log to clear a fire line. Hotshots are part of a highly skilled and well-trained team where each member has a specific job.

The hotshots also got their Pulaskis. Pulaskis have an ax at one end and curved metal at the other. They cut the fire line down to **mineral soil** on both sides of the fire. When spot fires **ignited**, they put them out. The crew was exhausted. But they worked as a team. Each member had a specific job. Some were **lookouts**. They watched for fires. Some were sawyers. They used chain saws to cut down trees. Swampers removed the limbs.

Then a tree fell. It hit a member of the hotshot crew! He was knocked out. A squad of five hotshots hiked back down the line. They got medical equipment and a backboard. A backboard is a flat, stiff board that keeps people still while they are being carried. They carried it up to the hurt crew member. He was being looked after by an **emergency medical technician** (EMT) on the hotshot crew. EMTs are trained to handle medical problems. The crew took turns carrying their hurt member safely back down the line. Then they went back to fight the fire.

The radio crackled to life. The wind picked up. The fire was coming. The crews' escape route had been cut off! They were trapped. But the hotshots stayed calm. They quickly backed down the line. Then they arranged their **fire shelters** in a tight circle. A fire shelter can withstand temperatures of 2,000 degrees Fahrenheit (1,093 degrees Celsius) for a couple minutes. They covered themselves. They called out to one another. They wanted to make sure their hotshot brothers and sisters were OK.

The hotshot crew came out of their shelters. They were fine. This had just been practice. It was part of the training and certification required to become a hotshot. The crew passed. They were ready to fight fires together for another year.

Chapter 4

INTO THE BLACK

Wildfires need three things: a spark, fuel, and wind. It was probably lightning that started the first fire. And there were plenty of trees for fuel in the Sierra Nevada Mountains. But the dry winds didn't help. They blew across California in September of 2020. They sparked 37 more fires across the northern part of the state. The fires launched pine cones and needles, igniting grass and **underbrush**. Entire towns were in the path of the fires. Firefighters were spread thin. The Truckee Hotshots were called in to help.

Superintendent Scott Burghardt had lots of experience. He knew when to go forward and when to go back. But today he wasn't sure. "There's not a real plan," he said. "We'll try to come up with a plan, pick up the pieces wherever we can."

First, the hotshots needed to clear the underbrush. This would deprive the fire of fuel. They got their chain saws and started cutting down young trees. Dustin Friedman had been a hotshot for seven years. He went down a hill called Devils Gap. He wanted to see where the fire was going.

◄ **Thick smoke and wind can make it more difficult and dangerous for hotshots to do their jobs.**

▲ **Wildland firefighters put out hot spots in areas that have already burned.**

He crossed the short flames and entered the black. The black is the area that has already burned. He wanted to show a helicopter pilot where to drop water. He flashed a strobe light (a flashing light) to get the pilot's attention. Dustin started looking for a place he could cross the fire to return to his crew. But the winds picked up. The fire heated up. He couldn't see because of the smoke. He would have to stay where he was for now.

Dustin hopped back and forth. The black ground was too hot to stand in one place for long. The chief radioed him to come back. But Dustin said he would have to stay for now.

Dustin looked at his phone's map. He could see where he was. But he couldn't see the fire because of the smoke. He kept moving his feet. He used his hand tools to scrape away ash. Ash would be cooler to stand in. But that didn't work. The soles of his boots melted. He poured water on them to cool them. After two hours, the chief found Dustin and led him out of Devils Gap. Dustin was taken to a hospital to be checked out. It was six weeks before he returned to the fire line.

THINK ABOUT IT

- What do you think are the best and worst parts of being on a hotshot crew?

- Hotshot crews face many risks. Why do you think men and women join hotshot crews? What personal characteristics are most important for crew members?

- Would you like to be part of a hotshot crew? Why or why not?

GLOSSARY

drip torches (DRIP TORCH-ez): A drip torch is a handheld tool to start fires. Hotshot crews use a drip torch when they need to burn small areas to help stop a large wildfire from spreading.

emergency medical technician (ih-MUR-jun-see MED-ih-kul tek-NIH-shun): An emergency medical technician, or EMT, is a person who provides medical care in an emergency. Many firefighters are also EMTs.

fire shelters (FIRE SHEL-turs): A fire shelter is a special heat-resistant tent used to protect firefighters. Hotshot crews always carry a fire shelter to use in an emergency.

ignited (igh-NITE-ed): To ignite means to set on fire. Burning pine cones and other plant materials can ignite fires.

lookouts (LOOK-owts): A lookout is a person who keeps watch. Some members of a hotshot crew are lookouts, while others clear away dead tree branches.

mineral soil (MIH-nuh-rul SOY-uhl): Mineral soil is the top layer of the earth's surface where plants grow. Firefighters clear the ground to the mineral soil when they make firebreaks.

remote (rih-MOHT): A place that is far from people is remote. Members of hotshot crews fight fires in remote areas.

terrain (tuh-RAYN): Terrain is a stretch of land. Firefighters in wildland areas are prepared to work in different types of terrain.

underbrush (UHN-dur-brush): Underbrush means small trees and bushes growing under big trees in a forest. Hotshot crews often clear away underbrush to prevent flames from spreading in a wildfire.

TO LEARN MORE

Books

Murray, Laura K. *Wildland Firefighter*. Mankato, MN: Creative, 2018.

Spilsbury, Louise. *Forest Fire Creates Inferno*. New York, NY: Gareth Stevens, 2018.

Westmark, Jon. *Smoke Jumpers in Action*. Mankato, MN: The Child's World, 2017.

Websites

Visit our website for links about hotshot crews: childsworld.com/links

Note to Parents, Teachers, and Librarians: We routinely verify our Web links to make sure they are safe and active sites. So encourage your readers to check them out!

SELECTED BIBLIOGRAPHY

Fire Science Degree Schools. "How to Become a Wildland Firefighter—Training Schools, Salary & Jobs." www.fire sciencedegreeschools.com.

Kramer, Melody. "Who Are the Hotshots? A Wildland Firefighting Primer." *National Geographic*. July 2, 2013. www.nationalgeographic.com.

Langellier, Robert. "Just Tell Me When I'm Going Home." Yahoo! News. December 16, 2020. https://ph.news .yahoo.com.

Whittaker, Max. "The Tools They Carry: Wildland Firefighters' Most Important Gear." *Outside*. www.outsideonline.com.

INDEX

ABOUT THE AUTHOR

Jody Jensen Shaffer is an award-winning poet and the author of more than 80 books of fiction and nonfiction for children. She lives in Missouri with her family.